Original title:
The Still Solstice

Copyright © 2024 Swan Charm
All rights reserved.

Author: Sebastian Sarapuu
ISBN HARDBACK: 978-9908-1-1543-6
ISBN PAPERBACK: 978-9908-1-1544-3
ISBN EBOOK: 978-9908-1-1545-0

Universe at Rest

Stars twinkle like diamonds bright,
In the calm of the velvet night.
Whispers of joy fill the air,
As the world pauses, with love to share.

Moonbeams dance on tranquil streams,
Laughter echoes, weaving dreams.
Soft breezes carry sweet delight,
In the universe's embrace, so right.

A Dance of Shadows

Underneath the crescent glow,
Shadows sway with a gentle flow.
Festive hearts beat as one,
In the magic of the night begun.

Candles flicker, casting light,
Creating joy, pure and bright.
Whirling leaves in a playful spree,
Celebrate the night, wild and free.

Gentle Quietude

In the hush of evening's balm,
Nature's peace is a healing charm.
Soft notes from a distant choir,
Lift our spirits, like fire.

Warm smiles shared in the night,
Hold close our dreams in soft light.
The world hums a sweet refrain,
In gentle quietude, joy remains.

In the Heart of Stillness

In stillness, laughter finds its place,
Wrapped in warmth, we share our space.
Colors burst in a vibrant hue,
As joy dances in all we do.

Gathered round, the stories flow,
Hearts alight with a warm glow.
In the heart where hope ignites,
Together, we create festive nights.

Whispers of Winter's Embrace

Snowflakes dance in the soft twilight,
Candles flicker, a warm invite.
Joyful laughter fills the air,
Hearts aglow, worries rare.

Mittens snug and spirits bright,
Families gather, a pure delight.
Songs of cheer in every space,
Love and warmth all interlace.

Silent Echoes of the Longest Night

Starry skies, a canvas wide,
Whispers of hope in the frosty tide.
Joyful cravings for sweet delight,
Gather 'round, hearts feel light.

Chill in the air, yet laughter flows,
Stories shared as the cold wind blows.
Unity drapes like a velvet cloak,
In the night, we bond and evoke.

Shadows Beneath the Frosted Stars

Moonlit pathways, soft and bright,
Shadows dance in the silver light.
Gifts wrapped tight with bows that gleam,
In the stillness, we dare to dream.

Fires crackle, the night ignites,
Sipping cocoa, feeling right.
Voices rise in joyous refrain,
In this moment, we break the chain.

Solitude in the Heart of Darkness

Frosted windows, quiet peace,
Solitude, yet joy won't cease.
Solemn whispers of sweet delight,
Hope emerges in the longest night.

Candles flicker, warmth ignites,
Faces glow in soft twilight.
Through the dark, our spirits soar,
In solitude, we find much more.

The Quiet of Ancients

In whispers soft, the ancients speak,
Their tales of joy, so rich, unique.
Laughter dances in the air,
A festive heart, beyond compare.

Underneath the starry sky,
Chants and songs from days gone by.
With every beat, the drums resound,
In every soul, the joy is found.

Colors burst in vibrant cheer,
Celebrations drawing near.
The fire's glow, a warmth so bright,
Guides the spirits through the night.

Unity weaves a tapestry,
Of love and peace, a symphony.
Hand in hand, we weave our dreams,
In festive laughter, life redeems.

Reverie of Dusk

As twilight drapes its velvet hue,
The world awakes, refreshed and new.
Candles flicker, shadows play,
In this moment, we wish to stay.

Festive bells begin to chime,
Carols sung in perfect rhyme.
Joyful hearts in unison,
Dancing 'neath the setting sun.

Friends and family gather near,
In their laughter, all sincere.
With every toast, a memory made,
In the warmth of love, we're arrayed.

The night unfolds its magic song,
In reverie, where we belong.
Fireflies twinkle, spirits soar,
In festive bliss, forevermore.

Night's Gentle Embrace

Stars twinkle softly in the sky,
Laughter dances, spirits fly.
Moonbeams cast a silver light,
In this warm and joyous night.

Friends gather round with hearts so true,
Stories shared in the joyful hue.
Chiming laughter, glasses raised,
In this moment, we are amazed.

Stillness Wrapped in Time

Candles flicker, shadows sway,
Whispers linger, night and day.
Warmth of fire, crackling cheer,
Hope and love can draw us near.

Clock ticks slowly, moments blend,
In this hush, we mend and tend.
With every heartbeat, life does hum,
In stillness, joy and peace will come.

Echoes of Winter's Grace

Snowflakes twirl in soft descent,
A tapestry of joy is lent.
Children's laughter fills the air,
Winter's charm is everywhere.

Fireside warmth on frosty nights,
Shared cookies, and holiday sights.
Echoes of merriment abound,
In this season, love is found.

Breath of the Chill

Whispers of winter, crisp and bright,
Nights adorned with stars' soft light.
Breath of chill upon our cheeks,
In cozy nooks, no one seeks.

Hearts ignite with stories told,
Friendship's warmth, a treasure gold.
With each hug, the chill takes flight,
In this moment, pure delight.

Gentle Fold of Snow

A gentle fold of snow arrives,
Soft whispers dance from winter skies.
Children laugh and spirits soar,
Joy lights up the earth once more.

Warm fires crackle, hearts aglow,
Kindred spirits share the show.
Mittens clapping, cocoa sipped,
In this wonder, time has tripped.

Twirling snowflakes, dreams take flight,
Moonlight twinkles, pure delight.
On this canvas, joy is drawn,
A festive spirit, winter's dawn.

In cozy homes, warm songs arise,
Glowing laughter, starry eyes.
In the gentle fold of snow,
Hope and magic freely flow.

Celestial Pause

Stars ignite the velvet night,
In a celestial dance of light.
The world below, a hushed embrace,
As dreams unfold in time and space.

Candles flicker, wishes cast,
Echoes of joy, forever last.
Underneath the twinkling glow,
Hearts connect, love starts to grow.

Carols rise in festive cheer,
Songs of laughter, drawing near.
In every corner, spirits bloom,
In the night, there's no more gloom.

With every gaze up at the sky,
We celebrate, we laugh, we sigh.
In this celestial pause, we know,
Together now, we let it flow.

Shimmering Silence

A shimmering silence cloaks the night,
As stars above grant softest light.
Footsteps crunch on frosty ground,
In every heartbeat, joy is found.

Trees adorned with sparkling white,
As laughter echoes, pure delight.
Children's faces all aglow,
In the magic, wonder grows.

The air is crisp, with cheer it sings,
A season blessed with joyful things.
In chilly breezes, memories weave,
Moments shared, on this eve.

With love wrapped tight, the world feels right,
In shimmering silence, dreams ignite.
Together in this festive glow,
Hearts entwined, we let it show.

Beneath the Winter Veil

Beneath the winter veil we roam,
In frosty fields, we carve our home.
With laughter bright, we chase the day,
In warm embraces, we love to play.

The world spins, cloaked in white,
Every heart feels pure delight.
From twinkling lights, a soft embrace,
In every shadow, joy we trace.

Gathered close, with hearts so true,
We sing our songs, both old and new.
Bells are ringing, spirits soar,
In this season, we ask for more.

Underneath the starry skies,
With wonder in our joyful eyes.
Beneath the winter veil, we share,
The festive magic, everywhere.

Ghosts of Light in the Dusk

Golden hues dance in the skies,
As twilight whispers soft goodbyes.
Stars twinkle like laughter's glow,
In the embrace of night's gentle flow.

Flickering lanterns sway with cheer,
Gather friends, pull each other near.
Songs of joy fill the chilled air,
Echoing dreams beyond compare.

Shadows twirl in festive delight,
While memories take flight at night.
Ghosts of laughter, hearts' sweet song,
In this warm glow, we all belong.

The Tranquil Pulse of the Earth

Beneath bright skies, the world does hum,
A tranquil beat, a gentle drum.
Nature sings in vibrant hues,
As dawn breaks softly with its cues.

Fields adorned in colors bright,
Chasing shadows, welcoming light.
Lively spirits, all around,
In this calm pulse, joy is found.

Children's laughter paints the scene,
Dancing through the grass so green.
Celebration in each breath,
Life's sweet song, defying death.

Lullabies of the Icebound Spirit

Under the blanket of winter's sheen,
Soft lullabies in the crisp serene.
Stars shimmer like dreams on the snow,
Guiding hearts wherever they go.

Frosty whispers weave through the trees,
As the night sings with a gentle breeze.
Icicles glisten, like diamonds bright,
In the embrace of the moon's soft light.

Gather close, let warmth abound,
In this magical, silent ground.
Dreams unfurl in the cold night air,
Festive spirits everywhere.

The Secret Weight of Darkness

In the hush of night, secrets play,
Wrapped in shadows, they find their way.
A candle flickers, casting glows,
Revealing tales of life's ebbs and flows.

Laughter echoes in hidden nooks,
As darkness wears its best outlooks.
Stars wink playfully from above,
Whispering tales of strength and love.

Under the cover of the moon's embrace,
Festive hearts find their rightful place.
In the weight of night's gentle fold,
The stories of life begin to unfold.

Eclipsed by Calm

In the light of golden cheer,
Joyful laughter fills the air.
Colorful lights twinkle bright,
Hearts unite in pure delight.

Dancing shadows on the ground,
Rhythms echo all around.
Voices lift, a sweet refrain,
Together, we break every chain.

Songs of love and dreams alive,
In this moment, we all thrive.
Beneath the stars, we find our way,
Eclipsed by calm, in joy we stay.

Where Night and Day Hold Hands

In the twilight's soft embrace,
Colors blend with gentle grace.
Fireflies dance, the stars ignite,
Whispers echo through the night.

Bubbles rise in sweet delight,
Celebrations glow so bright.
Together, laughter fills the space,
Where night and day find their place.

Candles flicker, shadows play,
Hope and joy pave the way.
With every heartbeat, spirits soar,
Unified in love we adore.

Reflections in a Crystal Pond

Rippling dreams on waters still,
Where the heart can freely spill.
Nature's joys and colors blend,
In this moment, we transcend.

Stars reflect like scattered pearls,
Whispers dance in rhythmic twirls.
Every splash a tale to weave,
Here in magic, we believe.

Evenings draped in silken hues,
Guiding us with painted views.
A canvas bright, where hearts respond,
Gathered near the crystal pond.

A Haven in the Depths of Winter

Snowflakes fall, a gentle kiss,
Blankets white, a scene of bliss.
Fires crackle, warmth ignites,
Joyful hearts through cozy nights.

Chilling winds may softly call,
But inside, there's warmth for all.
Crafting dreams with every breath,
Life and laughter conquer death.

Mugs of cocoa, laughter shared,
In this haven, all are bared.
Through the frost, our spirits rise,
Finding joy beneath the skies.

Lanterns in the Dark

In the night, soft lights glow,
Lanterns dancing, they flow.
Whispers of joy fill the air,
Guiding hearts, everywhere.

Life ignites with vibrant cheer,
Echoing laughter, drawing near.
Stars above join the parade,
In this warmth, all fears fade.

Moments of Tranquility

Gentle breezes through the trees,
Moments wrapped in sweet ease.
Candles flicker, soft and bright,
Whispers of peace in the night.

Gathered friends share a smile,
Time drifts by, a precious while.
In these pauses, hearts align,
Treasured bonds that brightly shine.

Luminous Silence

In the hush, a glow unfolds,
Silver secrets softly told.
Moonlight bathes the world in grace,
In this silence, dreams embrace.

Sparkling stars in the vast dome,
Guiding souls to their true home.
Moments wrapped in quiet bliss,
In this stillness, we find kiss.

Dreaming Beneath the Frost

Under blankets, warm and tight,
Dreams take flight in the night.
Snowflakes dance, a pure delight,
Painting worlds in shimmering white.

Whispers of warmth and cheer soar,
Hearts ignited with tales of yore.
In the frosty air we play,
Together, we'll chase winter away.

Contemplation in the Cold

Snowflakes dance with glee,
Laughter fills the air,
Warmth of hearts unite,
Joy beyond compare.

Candles flicker bright,
In the chilly night,
Whispers of the light,
Sparkle in delight.

Stories shared by fire,
Chasing away the dark,
Dreams that never tire,
Each one leaves a mark.

Together we will sing,
Underneath the stars,
Celebration's ring,
No matter where we are.

Tranquil Vale

Gentle breezes sway,
In fields lush and green,
Nature's grand ballet,
A peaceful, perfect scene.

Flowers bloom with pride,
Colors bright and bold,
In this tranquil tide,
Beauty to behold.

Laughter in the air,
Echoes soft and sweet,
Moments that we share,
With friends we like to meet.

Underneath the sky,
As day turns to night,
Happiness is nigh,
In the fading light.

Still Waters of the Night

Ripples softly glide,
Moonlight on the lake,
In this blissful tide,
Gentle waves awake.

Stars above us gleam,
As dreams take their flight,
In a tranquil dream,
We dance through the night.

Whispers in the dark,
Secrets that we keep,
In the soft and stark,
Where shadows seem to leap.

Hearts entwined as one,
In this peaceful scene,
Underneath the sun,
Where love's light will beam.

Soft Embrace of Solitude

A quiet retreat,
Where the world fades away,
In moments discreet,
Here I wish to stay.

With a book in hand,
Lost in tales so bright,
In a dreamlike land,
Wrapped in pure delight.

Time flows like a stream,
Gentle and serene,
In this perfect dream,
Where joy is seen.

Finding peace within,
In this sacred space,
Let the world begin,
With a warm embrace.

Pause Before Dawn

A soft glow whispers light,
In the hush of early air,
Laughter dances in shadows,
As dreams begin to share.

Joy floats on gentle breezes,
Carry hopes on whispered sighs,
The world is poised in beauty,
With stars that wink and rise.

Secrets of the Quiet Hours

Moonlight spills like laughter,
On streets where stories weave,
In the silence, joys awaken,
As hearts begin to believe.

Fleeting moments of magic,
Twinkling lights in the night,
Every shadow holds a secret,
Nurtured in soft delight.

Serene Interlude

Calm waves of starlit chatter,
Fill the air with sweet refrain,
Each note a joyful echo,
That's kissed by soft champagne.

Balloons float like dreams above,
Casting colors in the night,
A tapestry of laughter,
Joyful hearts in pure delight.

Gathering of the Stars

Stars gather in the twilight,
A parade of shimmering grace,
Their whispers weave a story,
Of joy that time can't erase.

Hear the echoes of the past,
As wishes take their flight,
In the warmth of celebration,
Every moment feels just right.

Beneath the Frosted Sky

Beneath the frosted sky we stand,
A world transformed by winter's hand.
With laughter ringing through the air,
We gather close, a joyful fare.

The twinkling lights like stars aglow,
Dance upon the fields of snow.
Each breath a fog, a whispered cheer,
In moments shared, we hold so dear.

The warmth of hearts, the chill dismissed,
In every hug, a warmth persists.
With feasting, games, and stories told,
Together we create pure gold.

So raise a cup to joy tonight,
Beneath the frost, our spirits bright.
For in this time, united we,
Embrace the magic, wild and free.

Moments Glazed in Ice

Moments glazed in ice, so rare,
We hold them close, we breathe the air.
With every twinkle in the night,
The world is wrapped in softest light.

Snowflakes dance like music's flow,
On every branch, a crystal show.
Laughter echoes, fills the space,
As joy and warmth, we now embrace.

The fire crackles, sparks take flight,
We gather 'round with hearts so bright.
In stories shared and songs we'll sing,
These moments, oh, what joy they bring.

So here we stand, our spirits high,
In love and laughter, we rely.
With every heartbeat, let's rejoice,
In every moment, find our voice.

Time Takes a Breath

Time takes a breath, the night is young,
In starlit skies, our hearts are strung.
Whispers of joy in sparkling light,
Fill every corner of the night.

With friends around, our spirits soar,
By the fireside, we laugh and roar.
The world feels right, a seamless blend,
As we embrace what night shall send.

The magic twirls like snowflakes small,
Creating warmth that binds us all.
With every cheer, our voices rise,
In rhythms sweet like lullabies.

So let us dance beneath the moon,
In every heart, a joyful tune.
For time stands still in festive grace,
Together here, our happy place.

Veil of the Midnight Sun

Veil of the midnight sun we see,
A tapestry of light so free.
With colors bright, they fill the sky,
In every moment, spirits fly.

We gather close, our hearts so full,
In laughter's song, the world feels whole.
With every hug, a warmth we share,
In friendship's bond, we breathe the air.

The night unfolds with stories grand,
Embracing all, we take a stand.
For in this joy, we find our place,
In festive cheer, time leaves no trace.

So let us raise our voices high,
Beneath the veil, we will not shy.
For in this night, with hearts so bold,
We weave our dreams in threads of gold.

Night's Soothing Touch

The moonlight dances on the ground,
Whispers of joy all around.
Laughter rings through the gentle air,
A promise of magic, oh so rare.

Stars twinkle like diamonds bright,
Holding secrets of the night.
Friends gather close, hearts are free,
Underneath the grand canopy.

Sweet melodies fill the space,
Smiles and warmth, a soft embrace.
Memories woven, laughter shared,
In this moment, hearts declared.

Joyous hearts, a vibrant beat,
Each rhythm a festive treat.
With every cheer, let's raise a glass,
To nights like this, may they always last.

Chilled Elegance

In the twilight, a cool breeze flows,
Whispers of secrets the moon bestows.
Ice crystals glisten in the soft light,
A dance of dreams in the calm of night.

Chilled champagne in delicate flutes,
Laughter echoes, elegant pursuits.
Silken gowns in shades so bright,
Creating a canvas for pure delight.

Around the fire, stories unfold,
Tales of adventures, lively and bold.
The warmth of friendship, a cherished glow,
A night to remember, steadily flow.

Beneath the stars, dreams take flight,
Chilled elegance, a magical sight.
As the night lingers, joy we find,
In this celebration, hearts intertwined.

A Still Heart's Reflection

Amidst the noise, I find my peace,
In silent moments, worries cease.
The gentle hum of the world outside,
As laughter swirls, my heart's wide.

In flickering lights, I seek the calm,
A soothing rhythm, a gentle psalm.
Reflections glimmer in my mind,
Treasured fragments, joy defined.

Each smile shared adds to the glow,
In this festivity, love does flow.
No rush, just beauty in each gaze,
A still heart's reflection, a warm haze.

Here in the stillness, I discover the art,
Of holding each moment, pure from the heart.
In laughter and whispers, a timeless connection,
Finding true joy in my heart's reflection.

Serene Under the Stars

The night unfolds, a serene sight,
Stars are twinkling, pure delight.
Under the heavens, dreams arise,
With every glance, a new surprise.

Flickers of joy in the cool night air,
Bright laughter echoes, hearts laid bare.
Together we stand, in the moon's embrace,
Sharing our hopes in this tranquil space.

The world softens, a gentle embrace,
Time stands still, in this sacred place.
With every heartbeat, love ignites,
In the warmth of community, spirits take flight.

United we are, under stars so bright,
Finding the magic, in sheer delight.
Together we'll dance, till the dawn does break,
In the still of the night, memories we'll make.

Veil of Silence

In the twilight, laughter rings,
Festive hearts play, joy it brings.
Colors dance beneath the stars,
A night alive, free from scars.

Whispers echo in the night,
Sweet melodies take flight.
Gathered close, we share this cheer,
In the magic, we forget fear.

Bubbles rise, champagne flows,
Sparkling dreams, the night bestows.
As shadows twirl, and spirits soar,
We celebrate, forevermore.

In this moment, we unite,
Underneath the moon's soft light.
With open arms, we greet the dawn,
In this veil, our worries gone.

As the World Holds its Breath

The world pauses, time stands still,
Hearts aflame, with joyous thrill.
Beneath the starlit velvet skies,
Magic lingers, as hope flies.

With each cheer, a spark ignites,
In the dark, our laughter lights.
Voices merge in sweet refrains,
A tapestry of joy remains.

In the air, excitement hums,
As every beat of music drums.
Fingers clasped, we sway and spin,
In this dance, where dreams begin.

As the world breathes in our song,
We know together, we belong.
In this moment, bright and true,
The heart celebrates, me and you.

Night's Whispered Secrets

Beneath the stars, a secret shared,
In festive whispers, none prepared.
Each laughter echoes off the moon,
In shadows deep, where dreams are strewn.

A candle flickers, tales unfold,
Of vibrant hearts and nights of gold.
Time, it dances on the breeze,
As joy spills out with perfect ease.

The night wears magic like a crown,
With every twirl, we spin around.
Friendship blooms, and love ignites,
In the embrace of warm delights.

Let the secrets softly flow,
In glowing hearts, forever glow.
With every toast, the world feels bright,
In whispered tales that light the night.

A Pause in Eternity

In this moment, time stands still,
Echoes of laughter fill the chill.
Colors flutter like fireflies,
A memory stitched beneath the skies.

As we gather, joy abounds,
In every heart, true love resounds.
With every cheer, the stars align,
In this pause, the world is fine.

The night unfolds, a festive spell,
In every sigh, a story to tell.
Happiness wraps around our souls,
As the universe plays its roles.

In this timeless, cherished space,
We find our dreams in warm embrace.
With every heartbeat, we unite,
In this pause, our spirits ignite.

Timeless Night's Reverie

Beneath the stars that gleam and shine,
Hearts gather close in perfect time.
Laughter dances in the air,
Joyful whispers everywhere.

Candles flicker, casting light,
Shadows play on this sweet night.
Songs of love and dreams take flight,
In the warmth of pure delight.

Moments cherished, young and old,
Stories shared, as dreams unfold.
Together lost in time's embrace,
In this night, a sacred space.

As the midnight bell does chime,
We toast to love, and life, and rhyme.
Timeless memories we create,
In reverie, we celebrate.

Silent Zenith

At the peak of evening's grace,
Moonlight bathes the vibrant space.
Stars above begin to glow,
Whispers of the night, so slow.

Gathered close, with cheer we find,
Ties that bind, so sweet and kind.
Voices lift like winds in flight,
Singing softly through the night.

New tomorrows in our sight,
Joyful dreams ignite the light.
In the stillness, hearts unite,
Found in this serene delight.

Silent zenith, magic hums,
As the earth around us drums.
Forever bound in love's pure glow,
In this moment, hearts will grow.

Whispering Shadows

Underneath the twilight veil,
Softly sway the dreams we sail.
Gentle whispers fill the night,
Every star a beacon bright.

In the quiet, laughter's tune,
Colors dance beneath the moon.
Hearts entwined in sweet embrace,
Fleeting time, a sacred space.

Moonlit paths where echoes play,
Guide our hearts along the way.
In the stillness, hopes take flight,
Whispering shadows, pure delight.

Together we shall brave the night,
Hand in hand, our souls in flight.
Wrapped in warmth, we celebrate,
Life's embrace, it's never late.

Solace at Dusk

As the sun dips low and deep,
Golden hues in silence sweep.
Gather close, the evening sighs,
Underneath the painted skies.

Calm the heart, let worries cease,
In this hour, we find our peace.
Candles flicker, shadows gleam,
Time unwinds, a gentle dream.

With each laugh, a bond we weave,
In these moments, we believe.
Festive hearts, together sing,
Celebrating all life brings.

Solace found as day departs,
In our joy, we share our hearts.
Underneath the tranquil dusk,
Love's sweet essence, pure and husk.

A Time for Rest

In cozy corners, laughter blooms,
Bright candles flicker, dispelling glooms.
A tapestry of warmth and cheer,
In every heart, the joy draws near.

The table's set with treats galore,
Soft chatter hums, like waves on shore.
With every bite, a toast we raise,
To memories made in festive haze.

Outside the world may chill and freeze,
But here inside, we find our ease.
With songs that wrap us like a shawl,
Together we stand, together we fall.

As night drapes softly, dreams take flight,
In shared embraces, our spirits ignite.
The time for rest, for love, for play,
In this bright moment, forever stay.

Lantern Lights in Gathering Dark

Beneath the stars, the lanterns glow,
Casting shadows, dancing slow.
Each flicker whispers tales untold,
Of warm embraces and hearts of gold.

As laughter mingles with the breeze,
Joy unfurls upon the trees.
A blanket draped on soft, green grass,
Where time stands still, and troubles pass.

With every spark, a wish we share,
Filling the night with love and care.
Hand in hand, we chase the night,
In the magic of this glowing light.

As darkness wraps the world anew,
Together we find a hopeful view.
For in this place, our spirits soar,
Lantern lights guide us evermore.

Solitary Reverie

In quiet corners, thoughts unwind,
A world of dreams begins to bind.
Festive colors in silent flight,
A solitary heart takes flight.

With whispers soft, the breezes trace,
The echoes of a joyful space.
In simple moments, joys collide,
With memories cherished deep inside.

Against the night, where shadows play,
A canvas bright in disarray.
Each spark of joy, a flickering star,
Reminds us how close we really are.

Though solitude may softly call,
The heart remembers a merry thrall.
In reverie, the light stays true,
Festive spirits envelop you.

Frosted Whispers

With winter's breath, the world aglow,
Frosted whispers dance in the snow.
Each flake a gem from skies so high,
A shimmering world where dreams can fly.

In gatherings near, the warmth we share,
With mugs in hand, we breathe the air.
Laughter rings like bells in the night,
In every heart, a flickering light.

Tangled lights upon the tree,
Are reminders of you and me.
As stories weave through glowing eyes,
In this embrace, our spirit flies.

Let winter's chill not steal our zest,
In every moment, we feel the best.
Frosted whispers and cheerful songs,
Together we write where each heart belongs.

Shadows Dance in Stillness

Under the bright, flickering lights,
Shadows twirl in joyful flights.
Whispers of laughter fill the air,
As vibrant spirits clash with flair.

Colors burst like flowers in bloom,
In every corner, joy finds room.
With every heartbeat, rhythms play,
Festive echoes brighten the day.

Around the table, stories shared,
With every toast, love is declared.
A tapestry of dreams unfolds,
In this moment, warmth beholds.

Fireworks glitter in the night,
Under stars, the world feels right.
Hands are raised in sweet delight,
Together we dance into the night.

Quietude of the Heart

In the silence, peace takes flight,
Softly swaying, hearts ignite.
Beneath the moon's gentle embrace,
A tranquil joy we all can trace.

Candles flicker, shadows play,
Warmth and love guide the way.
Joyful whispers intertwine,
Filling spirits, sweet and divine.

Each moment draped in soft refrain,
Happiness blooms like springtime rain.
With every laugh, a bond is spun,
In the quiet, we're all as one.

So let the world fade away,
In this stillness, we shall stay.
Together in this lovely space,
Quietude brings a warm embrace.

Embracing the Quiet

A gentle hush enfolds the night,
In shadows soft, we find our light.
Moments linger, sweetly shared,
In stillness, our spirits are bared.

The world outside may roar and race,
But in this calm, we've found our place.
With whispers close, hearts intertwine,
In this quiet, we fiercely shine.

Laughter dances on the breeze,
Filling spaces with sweet ease.
Every smile a promise made,
In this embrace, worries fade.

So let us bask in tranquil dreams,
In the night, love softly beams.
Together we'll weave a tapestry,
Embracing the quiet, wild and free.

Echoes of the Ancients

In twilight's hue, the legends speak,
Whispers of old, softly sleek.
Around the fire, stories flow,
Ancestral echoes gently glow.

With every word, a heartbeat thrums,
In festive tales, nostalgia hums.
The past and present intertwine,
In these shared moments, we divine.

Under the stars, shadows dance bright,
In the warmth of hearts, all feels right.
Together we laugh, together we sing,
In echoes of love, our spirits take wing.

With drums that pulse, and voices that rise,
We celebrate under starlit skies.
In every echo, our spirits connect,
Forever bound, we shall reflect.

Elysium in Shadows

Underneath the twinkling stars,
Laughter dances on the breeze,
Joyful hearts weave tales anew,
In the night, our spirits seize.

Colors burst like fireworks bright,
Echoes of delight resound,
Together we create our dreams,
In this magical playground.

Candles flicker, warmth ignites,
Voices blend in sweet refrain,
Friendship blooms like springtime flowers,
Joy replaced with gentle pain.

As the night embraces all,
Hands entwined, we share this cheer,
In the Elysium we craft,
Memories cherished and held dear.

Whispers of the Faded Light

Among the shadows, whispers flow,
Glimmers of a bygone day,
Stories woven in the night,
Brightening the darkened way.

Candles glow, like tiny suns,
Lighting pathways near and far,
A celebration in our hearts,
Where dreams chase each shining star.

Footprints echo on the ground,
Dancing with a gentle sway,
In the stillness, laughter rings,
Guiding us to break of day.

Old tales rise on silver wings,
In the morn, they softly rest,
Faded light returns to shine,
Every moment, we feel blessed.

Harmony in Hibernation

Winter's chill brings us close,
Gathered 'round the crackling fire,
Songs of joy and tales of old,
Fuel the heart's eternal fire.

Under blankets, warmth we share,
Laughter dances in the air,
As the world outside turns white,
Within, we glow—a pure delight.

Frosty windows, pictures drawn,
Memories drifting, sweet and warm,
Together, we weave our dreams,
In this haven, love transforms.

Embracing moments wrapped in time,
In this hibernation's grace,
Harmony whispers in the night,
With every smile, we find our place.

Celestial Embrace

Under a sky of shimmering grace,
Stars aligned in grand display,
Together under cosmos vast,
In this dance, our souls will sway.

Galaxies twirl, in joyous flight,
While we trace the paths of light,
Hands held tight, we share our dreams,
In this festive, endless night.

Comets streak like wishes made,
Bringing hope and sweet delight,
In this embrace of all we are,
We find our place in purest light.

With laughter echoing through time,
In this moment, brightly shine,
Celestial ties forever strong,
In our hearts, the universe aligns.

Quietude's Hidden Song

In the stillness, joy unfolds,
Whispers of laughter, warm and bold.
Colors shimmer, bright and fair,
As hearts unite in the cool night air.

Melodies dance on the gentle breeze,
Echoes of moments, sure to please.
Under the stars, the world feels right,
Embracing the magic of the night.

Candles flicker, casting gold,
Tales of wonder, forever told.
Every glance a silent cheer,
Celebrating love, bringing us near.

With every heartbeat, spirits rise,
Beneath the dome of endless skies.
Quietude sings her hidden song,
In this tapestry where we belong.

Spheres of Silence

In spheres of silence, joy is found,
A canvas bright, where dreams abound.
Glimmers of hope, fluttering light,
Each moment precious, pure delight.

Gazing at lights that twinkle so bright,
Wishes whispered into the night.
Balloons afloat, colors in the sky,
Joyful laughter as hours fly by.

Festooned in ribbons, we twirl and sway,
Embracing the night till the break of day.
The air is electric, a vibrant beat,
In spheres of silence, our hearts compete.

Luminous echoes of mirthful cheer,
Tales of adventures, drawing us near.
With every hug and joyful sound,
In this embrace, our souls are found.

A Dance of Light and Shadow

In a dance of light and shadow's embrace,
We weave our stories, laughter and grace.
Sparkling moments, vibrant and true,
Each note a treasure, shared by few.

Twinkling stars in a velvet sky,
Whispers of dreams that soar high.
Glowing fireflies paint the night,
As hearts ignite with warmth, so bright.

A symphony plays in the cool night air,
Dancing together, without a care.
Joy spills over like wine in a cup,
United in rhythm, we rise up.

With every step, souls intertwine,
Creating memories, yours and mine.
In this waltz of light and shadow's glow,
We find our way, as the night flows.

Breathing in the Frozen Air

Breathing in the frozen air so clear,
A chill like magic, drawing us near.
Glittering snowflakes, a soft embrace,
Whispers of winter, a tender grace.

Laughter echoes in the frosty night,
Every moment feels pure and bright.
Hot cocoa steaming, sharing a smile,
Moments together, every mile worthwhile.

The world transformed under a blanket white,
Dancing shadows in the pale moonlight.
Hand in hand, we wander and roam,
Finding in the chill a sense of home.

In every heartbeat, warmth ignites,
Carving memories in winter's lights.
Breathing in deeply, we share this bliss,
In the frozen air, our hearts reminisce.

Veiled Illumination

In the night, the lanterns glow,
Colors dance, a vibrant show.
Laughter rings, the air so light,
Hearts entwine in pure delight.

Stars above twinkle with cheer,
Joy and love, both draw us near.
Families gather, hands held tight,
In this warmth, our spirits ignite.

With the music, voices soar,
Echoes of a time before.
Memories weave through the night,
Veiled in soft, enchanting light.

As we celebrate and sing,
Hope and peace the season brings.
Underneath the moon's embrace,
A festive glow upon each face.

Chasing Shadows in Solitude

In the quiet, whispers play,
Shadows flicker, dance and sway.
Moonlight bathes the world in dreams,
Solitude not always what it seems.

With each breath, the night unfurls,
Stars alive in twinkling swirls.
Chasing shadows, hearts take flight,
In the stillness, pure delight.

Crickets sing their gentle tune,
Beneath a sky adorned with stars and moon.
Worries fade, the world feels bright,
In our hearts, we find the light.

Embracing moments, soft and clear,
Finding solace, drawing near.
In solitude, we laugh and sigh,
Chasing shadows, you and I.

The Flicker of Distant Fires

Distant fires, a soft embrace,
Warming hearts in this vast space.
Crisp air carries stories old,
In the glow, adventures told.

Friends gather round, their laughter flows,
As the evening breeze gently blows.
Under stars, our dreams take flight,
In this moment, pure delight.

Sparks send whispers to the night,
Flames dance wild, a festive sight.
With each crackle, joy expands,
We find magic in our hands.

So we cherish, hearts aligned,
In the flicker, peace we find.
Memories made, both near and far,
Guided by the evening star.

Embers Beneath the Snow

Winter night, with stars aglow,
Whispers soft, like falling snow.
Beneath the frost, the warm hearts glow,
Embers dance in the moonlit flow.

Fires crackle, stories stir,
Laughter spills as spirits purr.
In each moment, hope takes flight,
Shining bright on this cozy night.

With each sip of cocoa sweet,
Friends and family gather, meet.
Chilled outside, but warmth within,
In the laughter, joy begins.

So let the world outside be cold,
Here, together, our hearts hold.
Embers glowing, love is near,
In the snow, we find our cheer.

Embrace of the Longest Night

Dancing lights twinkle high,
In the crisp and starry sky.
Joyful laughter fills the air,
Love and warmth are everywhere.

Feasting round a table bright,
Hearts unite in pure delight.
Softly glows the candle's flame,
In this night, we're all the same.

Whispers shared in cozy nooks,
Tales unfold like timeless books.
Wrapped in blankets, spirits soar,
In this magic, we explore.

Celebration knows no bounds,
In this joy, our bliss resounds.
Together we embrace the night,
In love's glow, everything's right.

Hushed Gleam

Moonbeams dance on frozen lakes,
A quiet charm that softly wakes.
Crimson flames in hearths alive,
In this peace, our spirits thrive.

Frosted whispers, secrets told,
Stories cherished, hugs to hold.
In the silence, hearts engage,
Living moments, turn the page.

Candles flicker, shadows play,
Warming souls in soft array.
In the hush, we find our cheer,
Every heartbeat draws us near.

A tapestry of joy unfolds,
With every smile, the magic molds.
In this glow, the world feels bright,
Wrapped in love's gentle light.

Twilight's Lullaby

As sun dips low, the sky ignites,
Softly swirling, festive sights.
Gathered close, we share a song,
Melodies where we belong.

Shadows stretch with evening's grace,
In warm hearts, a cherished space.
Glistening stars in velvet night,
Whispering dreams, a pure delight.

With every note, our spirits rise,
Echoes lifted to the skies.
In this twilight, time stands still,
Hearts united, pure goodwill.

Together here, we weave a tale,
Through laughter, love will never pale.
In twilight's embrace, we find our way,
Guided by the joy of today.

Frozen Reflections

Snowflakes drift in playful flurries,
Wrapping earth in winter's worries.
Each sparkle tells of sweet delight,
In this world, we're free to flight.

Glistening pathways spark our glee,
Bundled close, we roam with ease.
With cheers that echo, hearts awake,
In the chill, we dance and shake.

Fires crackle, warmth we share,
Stories spun with tender care.
In the frosty, joyous night,
Every moment feels so right.

Gather 'round the softly glowing,
In this bliss, our love is showing.
Frozen memories a cheerful sight,
In our hearts, eternal light.

Veil of Midnight

Stars twinkle bright in the cool night air,
Laughter and joy echo everywhere.
Lanterns sway gently, casting their glow,
As hearts dance lightly, like soft falling snow.

Chiming of bells rings through the trees,
Whispers of secrets in the soft, crisp breeze.
With every step, the magic unfolds,
A tapestry woven in vibrant golds.

All gather 'round, hands held so tight,
Fingers entwined, we embrace the night.
Singing and swaying, a beautiful sight,
Under the veil of the soft moonlight.

In this moment, we are truly free,
Wrapped in a warmth, like a sweet melody.
Together we shine, our spirits ignite,
In the embrace of the veil of midnight.

Surrender to Stillness

In the hush of the morning, peace paints the dawn,
Nature awakens, the world moves on.
Beneath the soft quilt of harvest's delight,
We surrender ourselves to the stillness of night.

Golden rays stretch, a warm, gentle touch,
Whispers of calm that envelop so much.
As leaves gently sway in the quiet parade,
We dance in the stillness, our worries allayed.

Candles flicker softly, casting their spell,
In the heart of the moment, all is well.
The world feels enchanted, wrapped up in grace,
As we revel in silence, find our true place.

Surrender to stillness, let go all aloud,
Float on the essence of dreams unbowed.
In the kinship of souls, our spirits align,
In the warmth of the moment, forever we shine.

Frosted Serenity

Soft flakes of white blanket the ground so pure,
Every breath a whisper, a promise, a lure.
Under a canopy of crystal and light,
We dance with delight in the heart of the night.

Frosted trees gleam with a magical sheen,
Like diamonds adorning a tranquil scene.
The laughter of children fills the cool air,
As joy spreads its wings without any care.

Each twinkle and sparkle, a wish waiting to soar,
In this winter wonderland, our spirits explore.
Building sweet dreams in the snowflakes' embrace,
Wrapped in the warmth of love's sweet grace.

Frosted serenity sings in our hearts,
In moments of magic where beauty imparts.
Together we revel, hand in hand we gleam,
Caught in the wonder of a silvery dream.

Celestial Calm

Under a blanket of stars, we drift,
Soft melodies dance, a gentle gift.
The world glimmers brightly, a dream in the air,
In the celestial calm, we find peace everywhere.

Moonlight cascades on the tranquil sea,
Whispers of night wrap around you and me.
With every heartbeat, the universe sings,
In this moment we share, our spirits take wing.

The night is a canvas, painted in hues,
Of midnight blues and soft golden views.
We glide through the silence, a beautiful flow,
As we soak in the magic that night tends to show.

Celestial calm reigns over the scene,
In the warmth of each breath, a sweet, tender dream.
Together we linger, in love we remain,
Bound by the stars in this sweet, soothing chain.

A Pause in Time's Breath

In laughter's echo, we unite,
Bright colors dance in soft twilight.
Around the fire, stories weave,
In this moment, we believe.

Candles flicker, shadows sway,
Joyful hearts lead the way.
With every cheer, the night grows bold,
A tapestry of dreams unfolds.

Hands raised high, spirits soar,
Together we ignite the floor.
The air is thick with sweet delight,
As we celebrate this vibrant night.

So let us pause, feel the grace,
In time's embrace, in love's space.
For in this world, we find our tune,
A symphony beneath the moon.

Nightfall's Gentle Caress

Stars twinkle like laughter shared,
In a blanket of night, we are ensnared.
The sky whispers secrets of old,
As tales of wonder and dreams unfold.

A soft breeze carries hopes anew,
Under the glow of the silver hue.
With friends beside, our spirits blend,
In this moment, we transcend.

Laughter dances on the air,
Echoes of joy, we freely share.
Together beneath the twilight's glow,
In this magic, our hearts know.

So let the stars be our guide,
In this festive night, with arms open wide.
For as the moon wraps us tight,
We bask in love's warm light.

Radiance of the Distant Sun

Golden beams break the dawn,
With each new day, our hopes are drawn.
Laughter spills like morning dew,
In the light, all feels brand new.

Colors burst in joyful cheer,
As we gather, loved ones near.
With hearts aglow, we lift our song,
In this moment, we belong.

The sun ignites our vibrant souls,
With every smile, our spirit rolls.
Festive echoes fill the air,
In unity, we find our care.

So let's embrace this morning bright,
With hands held tight, we dance in light.
For in the warmth of the sun's array,
We cherish love in every way.

Hushed Tales of the Frozen Moon

Beneath the moon's soft, silvery gaze,
We gather close, in warm arrays.
Whispers dance on the chill of night,
As starlit dreams take gentle flight.

Snowflakes twirl like laughter sweet,
Blanketing earth with a soft retreat.
In every flake, a story lies,
Of festive cheer beneath the skies.

Fires crackle, warmth ignites,
As shadows play in winter's sights.
With mugs raised high, we toast the night,
In joyful harmony, all feels right.

So as the moon watches above,
In this moment, we give love.
For in the hush, our stories bloom,
In the magic of the frozen moon.

Frost-Laden Dreams

Snowflakes dance in the golden light,
Children laugh, their cheeks so bright.
Hot cocoa warms their tiny hands,
As joy spreads wide across the lands.

Twinkling lights adorn the trees,
Whispers carried by the breeze.
Glistening roads, a sparkling show,
Where every heart feels the warm glow.

Songs of cheer fill the crisp air,
Echoing love and joy laid bare.
Merriment weaves through every street,
In this festival, life feels complete.

Frost-laden dreams in a winter's embrace,
Memories gathered, time can't erase.
Fireside tales told with delight,
We celebrate love on this starry night.

Quiet Beacons

Softly shines the winter moon,
Guiding hearts, a gentle tune.
Fires crackle, shadows sway,
Inviting warmth at end of day.

Blankets wrapped, we huddle tight,
Around the glow, our spirits ignite.
Laughter spills like melting snow,
Friendship's light begins to grow.

Carols rise with the evening star,
Voices blend from near and far.
Each note a beacon, bright and clear,
A festive reminder that love is near.

Cookies baked with joy and care,
The scent of magic fills the air.
Together we share this tranquil night,
In quiet beacons of shared delight.

A Timeless Interval

In snowy fields where silence reigns,
Time pauses, shedding all our pains.
Wrapped in warmth, we find a space,
To cherish each soft, lingering trace.

Beneath the stars, each twinkle gleams,
In this moment, we craft our dreams.
Hot cider hugs in frosty climes,
Creating laughter that transcends time.

Frosted windows, etched with art,
Holding memories close to heart.
Every heartbeat, a festive cheer,
Celebrating all we hold dear.

As night falls soft like a soothing balm,
A timeless interval, pure and calm.
We gather close, our spirits intertwined,
In this joyful pause, true peace we find.

Winter's Softened Breath

With every flake that graces the ground,
A gentle hush wraps all around.
Children play in the glistening snow,
Crafting dreams in frosty glow.

Mittens donned, lips painted red,
Warmed by fires where stories are spread.
Together we share warm, hearty meals,
As laughter dances, joy reveals.

Snowmen stand, proud and bright,
Guardians of our winter night.
Candles flicker, casting soft light,
In winter's breath, everything feels right.

As stars peek through the velvet sky,
In every moment, love amplifies.
We celebrate with every sigh,
In winter's embrace, we all fly high.

Enchanted Moments of Quietude

In twilight's gleaming, laughter sings,
As stars awaken, hope takes wing.
Soft whispers dance on the evening breeze,
Wrapped in magic, hearts find ease.

Flickering candles, a warm embrace,
Joyful faces, love we trace.
In stillness, dreams begin to bloom,
Every moment filled with room.

Branches swaying, the moonlight glows,
Sweet melodies in the night flows.
Together we share these gentle hours,
With every smile, love empowers.

In enchanted moments, we find our way,
In laughter and joy, life's bright display.
Each passing second, we come alive,
In this quietude, we truly thrive.

Beyond the Veil of Light

Beneath the stars, bright wonders gleam,
A tapestry woven from every dream.
In colors bold, the night ignites,
Together we dance, hearts taking flight.

Fireworks bursting in joyous delight,
Echoes of laughter fill the night.
As echoes fade, the music swells,
In every heart, a story tells.

Hands entwined, we chase the dawn,
Guided softly by hope reborn.
Beyond the veil, in unity,
We celebrate our harmony.

In festive moments, love takes flight,
As we journey on, a radiant light.
Together, we weave our dreams anew,
In this vibrant dance, just me and you.

The Stillness Between Breaths

In the stillness, joy whispers near,
With every heartbeat, love appears.
Together we pause, we share this grace,
In the silence, we find our place.

Golden lanterns sway in the air,
A symphony swirls, a rhythmic flare.
Moments captured, sweet and clear,
In this stillness, I hold you dear.

While the world rushes, we find our beat,
In gentle moments where souls meet.
As laughter echoes, a tender call,
In the quiet, we have it all.

Let time surrender, let worries cease,
In every silence, we find peace.
Together we breathe, together we spark,
In this stillness, our love leaves its mark.

Frost-Laden Dreams of Tomorrow

Snowflakes whisper on frosty eves,
As children gather, laughter weaves.
In dreams adorned, the world takes flight,
With every twinkle, hearts ignite.

Through icy paths, we trace our way,
In joyful moments, we laugh and play.
The warmth of fires, the glow of gold,
In stories of old, our dreams unfold.

With every heartbeat, hope ascends,
Holding each other, love transcends.
As tomorrow beckons, bright and clear,
In frost-laden dreams, we persevere.

Together we carve this tapestry,
In festive colors, wild and free.
With every dance under starry skies,
We cherish tomorrow with open eyes.

www.ingramcontent.com/pod-product-compliance
Ingram Content Group UK Ltd.
Pitfield, Milton Keynes, MK11 3LW, UK
UKHW021209231224
452712UK00006BA/639